Table of Contents

Hummingbirds

are some of the smallest birds in the world. There are more than 300 kinds of hummingbirds! Many hummingbirds live in South America. But some live in North and Central America, too.

Hummingbirds like to feed from bright flowers.

AMAZING ANIMALS

HUMMINGBIRDS

BY KATE RIGGS

CREATIVE EDUCATION • CREATIVE PAPERBACKS

Published by Creative Education and
Creative Paperbacks
P.O. Box 227, Mankato, Minnesota 56002
Creative Education and Creative Paperbacks are
imprints of The Creative Company
www.thecreativecompany.us

Design by The Design Lab
Production by Chelsey Luther and Rachel Klimpel
Edited by Alissa Thielges
Art direction by Rita Marshall

Photographs by Alamy (Stephen Brown), Getty
(Alexandra Rudge, Juan Carlos Vindas, Susan Gary,
Tier und Naturfotografie), iStock (Damocean), Pixabay
(Daniel Roberts), Science Photo Library (Dr P. Marazzi),
Shutterstock (BraulioLC, Martin Pelanek, Martina
Birnbaum, Pedro Bernardo, Wang LiQiang), SuperStock
(Minden Pictures, Radius)

Library of Congress Cataloging-in-Publication Data
Names: Riggs, Kate, author.
Title: Hummingbirds / by Kate Riggs.
Description: Mankato, Minnesota: The Creative
Company, [2023] | Series: Amazing animals | Includes
bibliographical references and index. |
Audience: Grades 2–3 | Summary: "Meet the small yet
mighty hummingbird! This book introduces these birds to
elementary kids, exploring their features and behaviors,
including their amazing flying abilities. A folktale explains
how hummingbirds got their colorful feathers"—Provided
by publisher.
Identifiers: LCCN 2021045148 (print) | LCCN
2021045149 (ebook) | ISBN 9781640265448
(hardcover) | ISBN 9781682770993 (paperback) |
ISBN 9781640007420 (ebook)
Subjects: LCSH: Hummingbirds—Juvenile literature. |
    Hummingbirds—Behavior—Juvenile literature.
Classification: LCC QL696.A558 R545 2023 (print) |
LCC QL696.A558 (ebook)
    | DDC 598.7/64—dc23
LC record available at https://lccn.loc.gov/2021045148
LC ebook record available at https://lccn.loc.
gov/2021045149

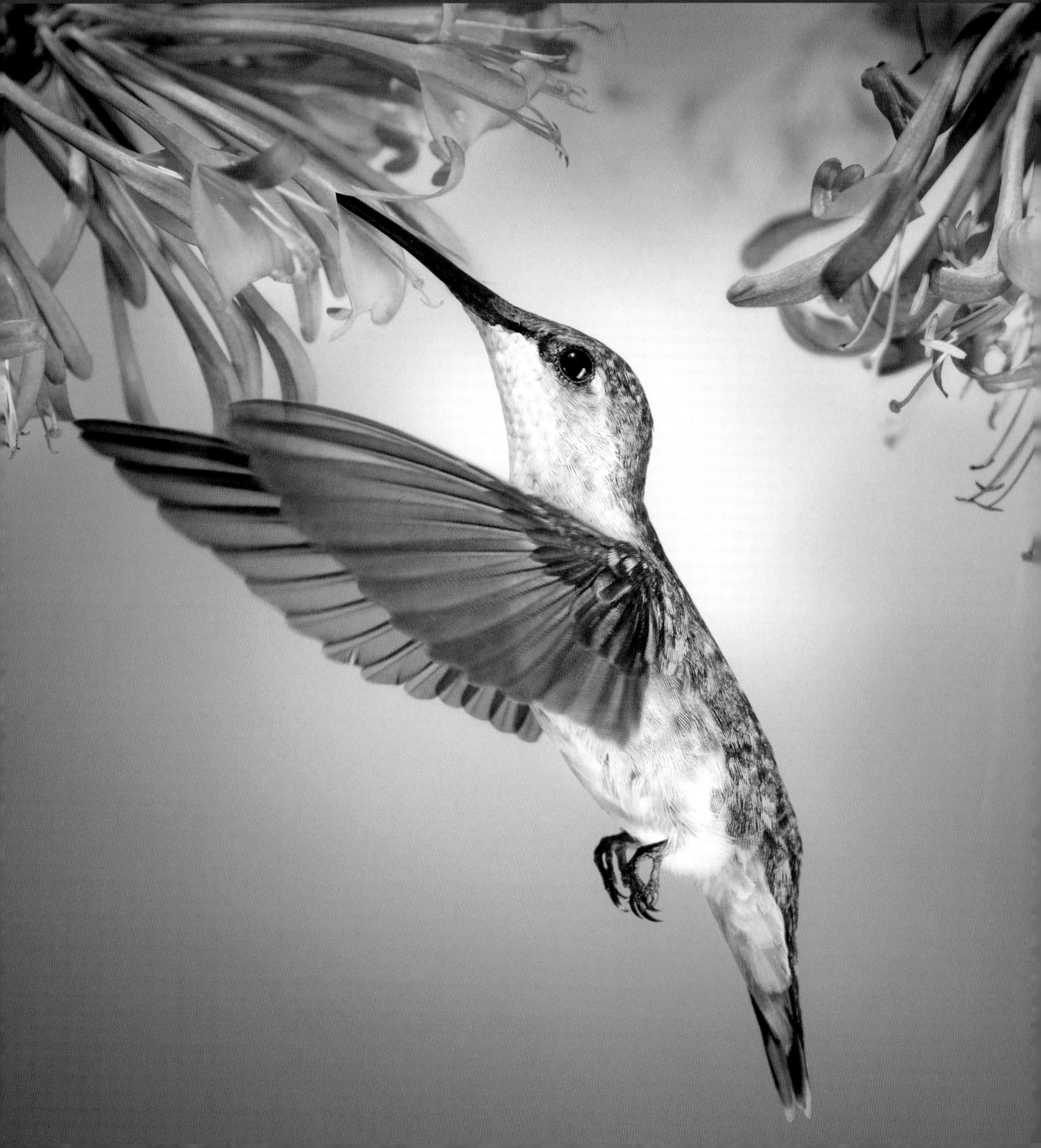

Hummingbirds have about 1,000 feathers on their body.

Hummingbirds

have colorful feathers. They have a long, pointy **beak**. Hummingbirds fly so fast that their wings make a humming sound. That is how they got their name.

beak the part of a bird's mouth that sticks out from its face

Bee hummingbirds (above) are the smallest birds. They weigh less than a penny! Even large hummingbirds do not weigh much. The giant hummingbird is the biggest hummingbird. It weighs about as much as six sheets of paper.

Giant hummingbirds live in western South America.

Fiery-throated hummingbirds live in forests in Costa Rica.

Most hummingbirds live in the warmest parts of the Americas. Many hummingbirds in North America **migrate** south in the winter. They go where they can find the most food.

migrate move from place to place to find food and warmth

Hummingbirds

eat insects and food from flowers. The **nectar** made by flowers is sweet. Hummingbirds need to eat a lot of sugary nectar. A hummingbird uses its curved beak and long tongue to reach the nectar inside a flower.

nectar a sweet, sugary liquid that flowers make

A hummingbird egg is less than 0.5 inch (1.3 cm) long.

A female hummingbird builds a nest before laying two to three eggs. She keeps the eggs warm until they **hatch**. Baby hummingbirds eat food their mother brings to them. The **chicks** leave the nest when they are about one month old.

chick a baby hummingbird

hatch break open

Many hummingbirds live about four to six years. Snakes and big birds called kestrels try to catch and eat hummingbirds. Hummingbirds live close to other hummingbirds. But they do not live together in families.

Hummingbirds scoot sideways but do not hop or walk.

A hummingbird flaps its wings 50 to 200 times per second.

Hummingbirds

feed and fly all day. They are the only birds that can fly in any direction. They fly up, down, forwards, and backwards. They can even **hover**! Hummingbirds eat a lot to fuel their fast flying.

hover stay in one place in the air

Sometimes you can see hummingbirds at special bird feeders. People can make a sugary water that hummingbirds like. It is fun to watch these colorful birds dart around!

Some feeders have spots for birds to perch while drinking.

A Hummingbird Tale

People in Mexico have a story about how hummingbirds got their beautiful feathers. The hummingbird used to be plain and gray. But she was cheerful and helpful. She had many bird friends. Her friends gave her some of their colorful feathers to make a wedding dress. The hummingbird loved the dress so much that she wore it forever. Hummingbirds are still some of the prettiest birds.

Read More

Gray, Susan H. *Ruby-Throated Hummingbird Migration*. Ann Arbor, Mich.: Cherry Lake Publishing, 2021.

Rajczak Nelson, Kristen. *Hummingbirds*. New York: Gareth Stevens Publishing, 2023.

Websites

Cornell Lab: Anna's Hummingbird
https://www.allaboutbirds.org/guide/Annas_Hummingbird/
Read cool facts about this hummingbird and listen to its sounds.

National Zoo: Hummingbirds
https://nationalzoo.si.edu/migratory-birds/hummingbirds
Find out the whys and whats of hummingbirds and the flowers they are attracted to.

PBS Nature: Secret of the Hummingbird's Tongue
https://video.idahoptv.org/video/nature-secret-hummingbirds-tongue/
Watch how hummingbirds drink flower nectar.

Note: Every effort has been made to ensure that the websites listed above are suitable for children, that they have educational value, and that they contain no inappropriate material. However, because of the nature of the Internet, it is impossible to guarantee that these sites will remain active indefinitely or that theirt contents will not be altered.